Naughty Edition

How to play?

This fun book is best enjoyed with with your partner at night, while on a road trip, or anywhere you both have lots of privacy. It could also be used as a fun drinking game involving more than one couple. It all depends on how close your married friends are to you, and the sorts of jokes you share.

Rules of play

The rules are simple. Your partner reads a question, and you proceed to answer the question. You have to answer the question, by choosing one of the choices in the book. You can't choose both choices at once or neither of them. Simply take turns going back and forth, while having fun. There is no winner or loser.

What you gain

This fun game opens a door, that most couples and people in relationship find hard to get through. It helps you see your partner through a non-biased lens, while exploring their hidden personalities. Topics you find hard to bring up, will easily come up, and it will suddenly be fun to discuss. This book will definitely get you both out of your comfort zone,

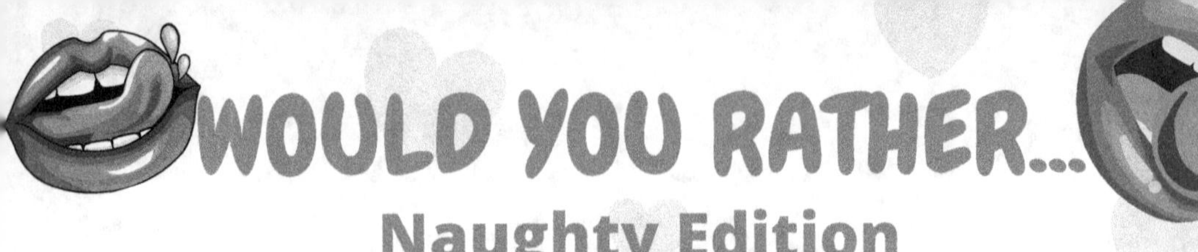

while planting a seed to make your relationship grow stronger. Most important of all, you will have lots of fun!!

Bonus tip

Make up your own rules for the game. E.g. You can come up with a very funny but true reason for making a choice. If it makes your partner laugh, you get a point. If it doesn't, you get no point, and vice versa. The person with the highest point at the end of 10 questions, gets to make a request that must be granted!

Another way to play the game, is to allow a limited number of follow up questions (e.g. 2), for each answer given (In this scenario, the answers given doesn't have to be funny). This will help to dig deeper into knowing the reasons your partner's choice of answer.

Disclaimer

WOULD YOU RATHER...

Have sex every hour of everyday

OR

Only when ready for bed at night?

Have 30 minutes of foreplay, and 5 minutes of sex

OR

5 minutes of foreplay, and 30 minutes of sex?

Watch an erotica movie

OR

Read an erotica novel?

Have a quickie in the bathroom

OR

In the car?

WOULD YOU RATHER...

Try something new and exciting in the bedroom with me

OR

Take up a new hobby together?

Have your hair pulled

OR

Your ass spanked?

Have a doggy sex style

OR

A missionary style?

Go skinny dipping alone in a pool

OR

With me in the ocean?

 # WOULD YOU RATHER... 

Give me a lap dance

OR

Have me give you a lap dance?

Watch porn with me, as part of foreplay

OR

Have me kiss you wherever you want?

Spit out my cum

OR

Swallow it?

Suck at foreplay

OR

Suck at sex?

# WOULD YOU RATHER...

Have me kiss your neck

OR

Your nipples?

I role-play as a cowboy/cowgirl

OR

As your favorite celebrity?

WOULD YOU RATHER...

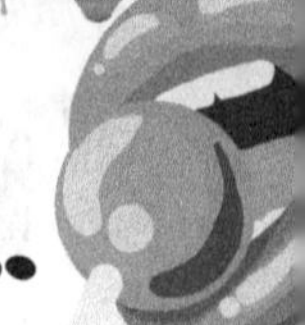

Go on a sex vacation in a cabin in the woods, just you and I

OR

In the Hedo hotel in Jamaica?

Be handcuffed during sex

OR

Blindfolded?

WOULD YOU RATHER...

Have the same sex position, all days of the year, but orgasm each time

OR

Try out new styles, every new day, but have no orgasm?

I french kiss you deeply

OR

Kiss you all over your body?

WOULD YOU RATHER...

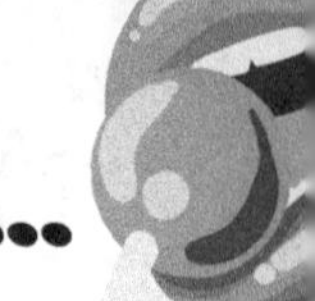

Suck my dick, until I cum into your mouth

OR

Have me cum someplace else?

Be restrained

OR

Do the restraining?

WOULD YOU RATHER...

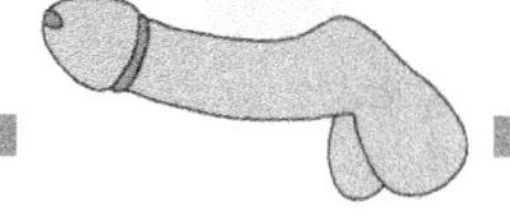

Have us look into each others eyes, while having sex

OR

Have our eyes closed?

Have sex with clothes on

OR

Without clothes on?

WOULD YOU RATHER...

Fantasize about steamy sex with your boss at work

OR

With a subordinate at work?

We have "romantic date night" more often

OR

"Fun date night" more often?

WOULD YOU RATHER...

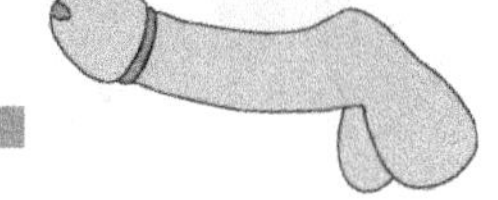

Have sex with the lights on

OR

With the lights off?

Never receive oral again

OR

Never eat your favorite food again?

WOULD YOU RATHER...

Sneeze every time you orgasm

OR

Orgasm every time you sneeze?

Walk around the house naked for a month

OR

Do the dishes and cooking for a month?

WOULD YOU RATHER...

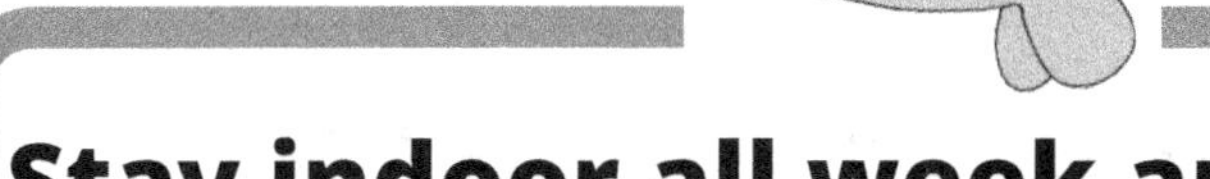

Stay indoor all week and have sex

OR

Go on fun romantic dates everyday, but no sex?

Never wear underwear again

OR

Never wear socks again?

WOULD YOU RATHER...

Go back in time, so you could experience having sex with me for the first time again

OR

Have sex with me, right now. I mean, right very now!

Get a naughty text from me, while you are at work

OR

A picture of me naked?

WOULD YOU RATHER...

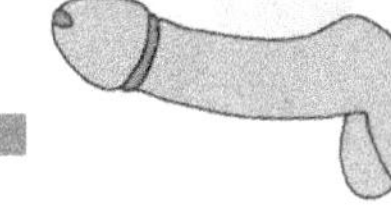

Have my penis in you for 1 hour straight

OR

Have me kiss you for that long?

Practise tantaric sex with me

OR

All the sex positions in the Kama Sutra?

WOULD YOU RATHER...

Explore the The Milk and Water Embrace sex position with me

OR

The Queen of Heavens?

Have your earlobes kissed gentley

OR

Your penis?

WOULD YOU RATHER...

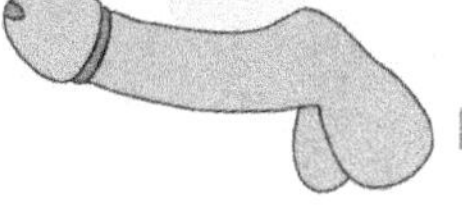

Have your neck kissed gentley

OR

Your clit?

Have a predictable sex life

OR

One full of surprises?

WOULD YOU RATHER...

Have an average sex that lasts 15 minutes

OR

An amazing sex that lasts 1 minute?

Only have sex in the shower

OR

Only on the floor?

WOULD YOU RATHER...

Have sex in complete silence

OR

While hearing dirty talks in an accent you don't like?

Be my sex slave for 2 weeks

OR

Stay celibate for 4 weeks?

WOULD YOU RATHER...

Have sex with me, and get arrested

OR

Never get to meet me, and stay safe all your life?

Watch me striptease for 1 hour, but no touching

OR

Touch me for only 1 minute, but no penetration or oral sex?

WOULD YOU RATHER...

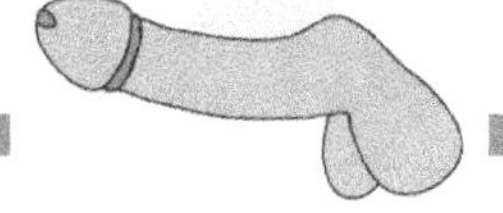

Post your nudes on social media

OR

Be a stripper for a night?

Have phone sex with me, after a month of not seeing

OR

Wait for me to get back home?

WOULD YOU RATHER...

Have me dance naked in front of you

OR

Talk dirty with you?

See me shirtless forever

OR

Pant-less?

WOULD YOU RATHER...

Watch porn with me

OR

Read out loud erotica poems?

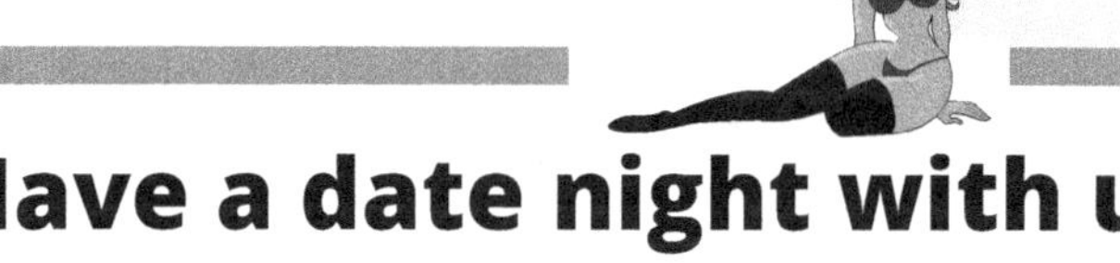

Have a date night with us as strangers meeting in a hotel

OR

With me as a pizza delivery man/lady?

WOULD YOU RATHER...

I pay you with more sex, for sex

OR

Take you for a special treat, for the weekend?

Watch me shower

OR

Watch me masturbate?

WOULD YOU RATHER...

Have sex, first thing in the morning

OR

After breakfast?

Have your lips kissed during sex

OR

Have your nipples sucked?

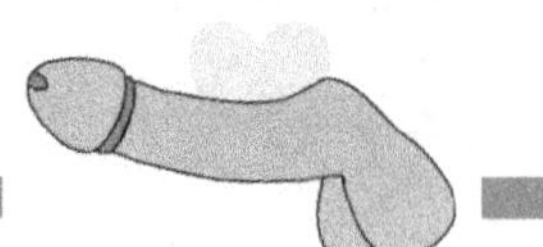

Whip

OR

Be whipped?

Have a cupboard full of sex toys

OR

Kinky outfit?

WOULD YOU RATHER...

Make out in a swimming pool

OR

On the kitchen table?

We have the house to ourselves on our anniversary

OR

Have family and friends over, and have a party?

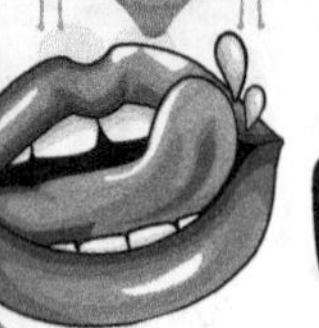

WOULD YOU RATHER...

I call/text you about how badly I want to fuck you

OR

Show you, by coming home, and fucking you whereever you are?

Make out in a mall's toilet

OR

On a beach?

WOULD YOU RATHER...

Give up sex

OR

Give up food?

Be better at sex than me

OR

Suck in sex, than me?

WOULD YOU RATHER...

Have a totally dominant partner

OR

A submissive one?

Have sex when you are drunk

OR

When you are very busy?

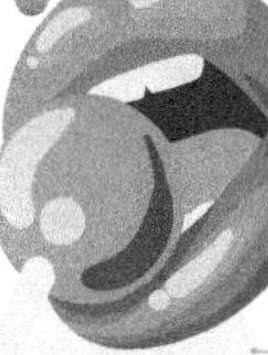

WOULD YOU RATHER...

Try out crazy new sex ideas

OR

Have slow, equally satisfying romantic sex?

Have sex everyday of the week

OR

Every other day of the week?

WOULD YOU RATHER...

Only have threesome, if you were single

OR

Never have sex?

Get dripped in chocolate pudding, and have me lick it as foreplay

OR

Have me pin you to the wall, and caress you?

WOULD YOU RATHER...

Wrestle in a bath tub filled with with melted chocolate

OR

Filled with honey?

I finger you under the table at a busy restaurant

OR

At the movies?

WOULD YOU RATHER...

Be teased with warm wax

OR

Ice cubes?

Have me dress up as a sexy doctor

OR

An exotic dancer?

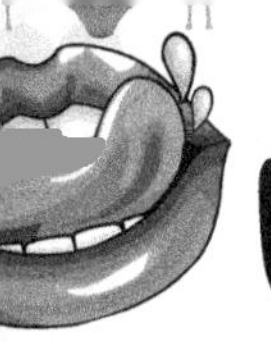

Have sex in 38°F weather

OR

100°F weather?

Cuddle in the morning

OR

In the evening?

WOULD YOU RATHER...

Sweat profusely during sex

OR

Moan loudly?

Fart in the while being given oral

OR

Belch while kissing?

WOULD YOU RATHER...

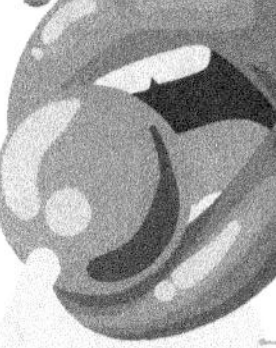

Be completely hairless

OR

Be covered in hair?

Feel vunerable around your neck

OR

Inside your thigh region?

WOULD YOU RATHER...

Have a 3 inches penis that stays hard for 30 minutes of sex, without cumming

OR

6 inches that stays hard for just 2 minutes, without cumming?

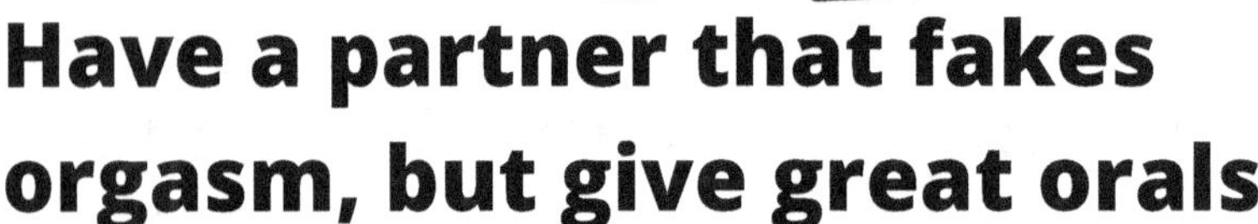

Have a partner that fakes orgasm, but give great orals

OR

Truly orgasm with a scream, but sucks at orals?

WOULD YOU RATHER...

Have a quickie in a secluded public park

OR

In an abadone public bulding?

Have a quickie with a 350 pounds hairy stranger, who then stalks you

OR

Passionate sex with a stranger, who then complains about your performance?

WOULD YOU RATHER...

Drive 200 miles to come fuck me

OR

Stay back home, and wait for me to return?

Have a year without the kids, but have a great sex life

OR

Have the kids around, but have sex only once a week?

 # WOULD YOU RATHER... 

Pay for sex

OR

Be paid for sex?

Fuck through a thunder storm, while hiding in the basement

OR

Sleep through it?

WOULD YOU RATHER...

Get turned on, by receiving gift from me

OR

Helping with whatever tasks you need done?

Mistakenly send your nudes to my friend

OR

To your boss?

WOULD YOU RATHER...

Initiate lovemaking

OR

Have me initiate it?

Have a "friend with benefits" relationship, if you were single

OR

Go for one night stands?

Fall asleep next to me

OR

Wake up next to me?

French kiss me in public once

OR

Text me you love me, every hour of everyday, for a week?

WOULD YOU RATHER...

Fall asleep after a good fuck

OR

Have me wake you up for sex?

We fuck at the dinner table after eating

OR

When we get back to the bedroom?

WOULD YOU RATHER...

Go to a strip club with me

OR

A boring symposium on the relativity of time?

Have meaningless one night stands

OR

A committed sexual relationship that can't last 8 month?

WOULD YOU RATHER...

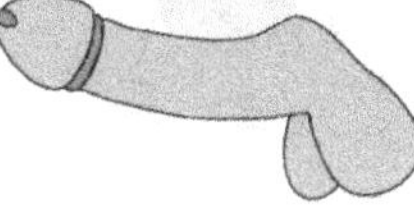

Be horny all the time

OR

Never be able to have an orgasm?

Have sex with someone very skilled in bed

OR

Someone very attractive?

Scream every time you have an orgasm

OR

Squeeze me tight to yourself?

Be with someone who loves to strip tease

OR

Tease with their lips?

WOULD YOU RATHER...

Have me wear seductive clothes around the house

OR

Walk around stark naked?

Have the whole of your penis in my mouth

OR

Have it licked like a lollipop?

WOULD YOU RATHER...

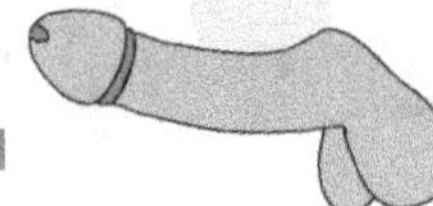

I never make you cum, no matter how long we fuck

OR

I never cum?

Fuck me on my desk at work

OR

In a parking lot?

WOULD YOU RATHER...

Always be horny

OR

Hardly be horny?

Have loud and rough sex while friends are visiting

OR

In a hotel room with thin walls, and your work colleagues are in the next room?

WOULD YOU RATHER...

Try out anal sex

OR

BDSM play?

Be blindfolded while receiving an oral

OR

Be restrained?

WOULD YOU RATHER...

Sniff my underwear

OR

Wear my underwear to work?

Watch porn with me

OR

Go to a strip club with me?

WOULD YOU RATHER...

Have a one night stand with your crush, if you were single

OR

A one night stand with a pornstar?

Get a handjob

OR

A blowjob?

WOULD YOU RATHER...

Make out with a married man/woman

OR

With a priest?

Never be able to have good sex again

OR

Good food again?

WOULD YOU RATHER...

Have your nipples gently licked

OR

Have it sucked?

Have the tip of your penis sucked

OR

The whole of your penis?

WOULD YOU RATHER...

We make our own porn, and watch it together

OR

Watch normal porn together?

Hear me moan heavily during sex

OR

Quietly?

WOULD YOU RATHER...

Fuck me when I'm drunk

OR

When I'm sober?

Have some music playing while we fuck

OR

Have everywhere be quiet?

WOULD YOU RATHER...

We start everyday with passionate sex

OR

End everyday with passionate sex?

Be more comfortable discussing our sex life with me

OR

Showing me what you don't like, while we are having sex?

WOULD YOU RATHER...

Date a sex addict

OR

Someone with a very low sex drive?

Eat my pussy

OR

Finger my pussy?

# WOULD YOU RATHER...

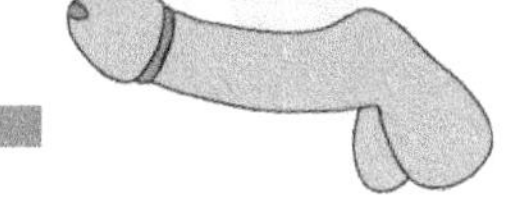

Watch lesbian porn

OR

Gay porn?

Enjoy sex better, with a clean shaved pubic region person

OR

A bushy pubic region person?

WOULD YOU RATHER...

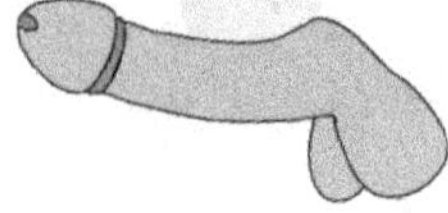

Date a pornstar

OR

Be a pornstar?

Grow shorter, each time you have sex

OR

Never have sex again?

# WOULD YOU RATHER...

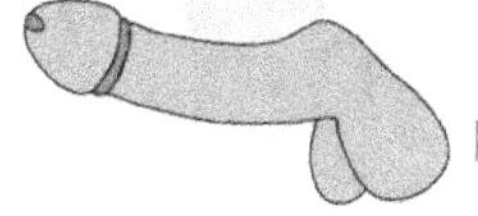

Walk nude on a busy street, to safe the world

OR

Watch the world burn?

Be with a partner you can't satisfy sexually

OR

A partner that can't satisfy you sexually?

WOULD YOU RATHER...

French kiss you with melted chocolate in my mouth

OR

Marshmallows?

Have great sex, but have to walk 3 miles every morning, before going to work

OR

Don't have sex for a whole month?

WOULD YOU RATHER...

Cuddle every time we are in bed

OR

Have us take a shower together everyday?

Have a video of you masturbating leaked on Facebook

OR

A video of you having sex?

WOULD YOU RATHER...

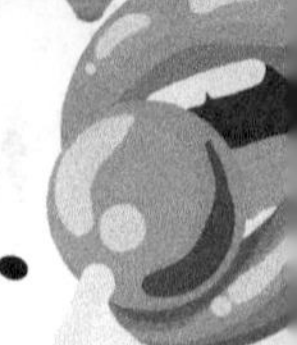

Fart uncontrollably when we having sex

OR

Scream your head off?

Talk dirty while having sex

OR

Be completely silent?

Have sex in an airplane's bathroom

OR

Get fingered in a library?

Know you don't please me in bed

OR

Spend your life in ignorance of it?

WOULD YOU RATHER...

Be a virgin until you are 60 years old

OR

Never be able to have sex after 60?

Have sex with someone that bites

OR

Someone that screams?

WOULD YOU RATHER...

Get very wet during sex that, the bed get soaked

OR

Squirt uncontrollably when you orgasm?

Have sex be messy

OR

Be careful and keep everything clean and tidy?

WOULD YOU RATHER...

Have sex on the couch

OR

In the backyard?

Have sex while standing up

OR

Lying down?

WOULD YOU RATHER...

Gain 300 pounds forever

OR

Lose your sex organ forever?

Have unlimited sex

OR

Unlimited money?

WOULD YOU RATHER...

Have sex without foreplay

OR

Foreplay without sex?

Be a prostitue

OR

A pimp?

Use a dildo in front of me

OR

Have me use it on you?

Eavesdrop on people having sex

OR

Pretend like you didn't hear anything?

WOULD YOU RATHER...

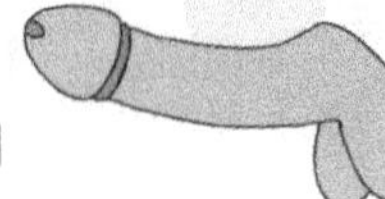

Have sex inside a car

OR

On the bonnet of the car?

Have a partner that takes forever to orgasm

OR

One that orgasm quickly?

WOULD YOU RATHER...

Get fuck from the back while bending over

OR

Ride my penis, while sitting on me?

Have me rub your penis while driving

OR

While you are watching a game?

WOULD YOU RATHER...

Receive a vibrator as a Valentine's Day gift

OR

A new phone?

Have your birthday cake be decorated with penises

OR

Dildos and other sex toys?

WOULD YOU RATHER...

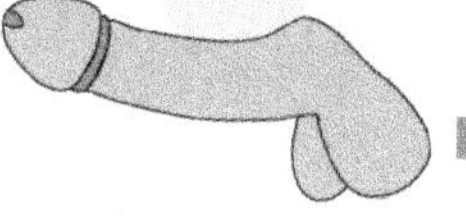

Be told you suck at kissing

OR

At giving blowjob?

Have sex in front of a police officer

OR

A live news taping?

WOULD YOU RATHER...

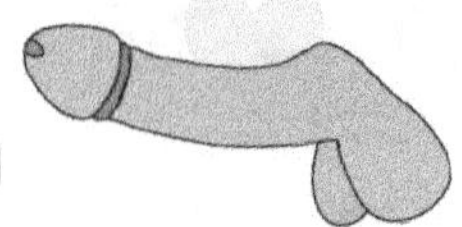

Be a sex addict, with lots of other sexual partners

OR

Be married to one?

Have sex with a celebrity you hate

OR

With your ex?

WOULD YOU RATHER...

Have a hickey on your cheek, each time we have sex

OR

A note pasted on your forehead stating "I Had Sex Last Night"?

Be turned on every time you see ice cream

OR

Every time you watch TV?

WOULD YOU RATHER...

Have me be secretly gay

OR

Secretly bisexual?

Get caught while having some freaky sex in your car

OR

While kissing a doll?

WOULD YOU RATHER...

Have sex while drunk

OR

While high on marijuana?

Attend a 30 minutes sex therapy session with me

OR

Go shopping with me for the whole day?

WOULD YOU RATHER...

Have more sex with me

OR

More foreplay?

Be offered a job as a pornstar

OR

As a stripper?

WOULD YOU RATHER...

Have no sex organ

OR

Two sex organs?

Experiment with more BDSM sexual activities

OR

Keep it vanilla, with no new experience?

WOULD YOU RATHER...

Get very horny, every time you see me

OR

Instantly have an orgasm?

I scream your name while having sex

OR

Give you kinky names?

WOULD YOU RATHER...

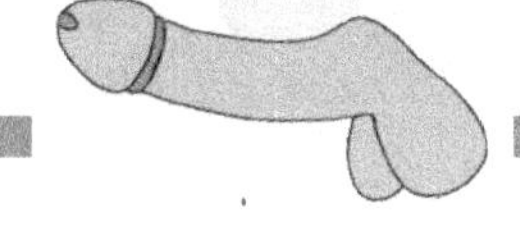

Have passionate sex while in the shower

OR

In the bath tub?

Make a funny face when you cum, and have it as your social media profile picture

OR

Make weird creepy noises, and have it as your phone's ring tune?

WOULD YOU RATHER...

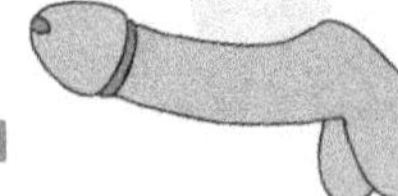

Spank my butt in public

OR

Grab my genital?

I don't move during sex, no matter how passionate we get

OR

I don't make any sound?

WOULD YOU RATHER...

Have bland sex, that always makes me fall asleep while in action

OR

Rough sex, that makes you feel bruised afterwards?

Have quickies before going to work every morning, everyday

OR

During break from work in the afternoon?

WOULD YOU RATHER...

Have a great relationship with an awful sex life

OR

A bad relationship with great sex life?

Be able to last an hour in bed

OR

Be able to make me cum anytime you want?

WOULD YOU RATHER...

Give a golden shower

OR

Receive one?

Have sex in a bed filled with stains

OR

A dirty bathroom floor?

WOULD YOU RATHER...

Cry every time we have sex

OR

Burp every time we kiss?

Wear a friend's dirty underwear

OR

Wear a G-string?

WOULD YOU RATHER...

Have sex without kissing me

OR

Without touching me with your hands?

Have a feminine voice

OR

A tiny dick?

# WOULD YOU RATHER...

Keep your shirt on during sex

OR

Keep your shoes on?

Have a one night stand with your celebrity crush

OR

A long term non-sexual relationship?

WOULD YOU RATHER...

Be a well known porn director

OR

A well know dark erotica novelist?

Be a cross dresser

OR

Have anal sex?

WOULD YOU RATHER...

Get turned on thinking of me as an exotic dancer

OR

As a model?

Have sex without touching my boobs

OR

Without touching my butt?

 # WOULD YOU RATHER... 

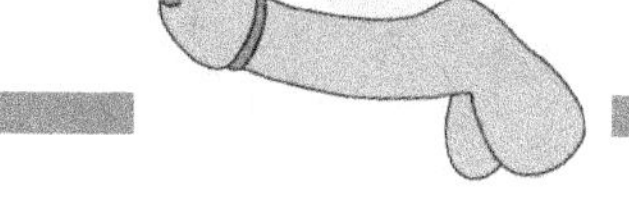

Have passionate sex so loud that the neighbors complained

OR

The bed get broken?

I talk to you dirty with a sexy French accent

OR

With an Italian accent?

WOULD YOU RATHER...

Have sex while watching tv

OR

While on a phone call?

I wear an outfit that shows my cleavage to seduce you indoors

OR

An outfit that shows my sexy ass?

 # WOULD YOU RATHER... 

Have a pussy that gets very wet and creamy while being fucked

OR

That queefs loudly?

Make me moan

OR

Make me laugh?

WOULD YOU RATHER...

Do a nude photo shoot with me, and have the pictures on our bedroom wall

OR

Wear something very revealing and sexy, for the photo shoot?

Have an intense make out session with a doll

OR

With a beautiful actress in a poster?

WOULD YOU RATHER...

Be on your kneels during sex

OR

On your back?

Read the 50 Shades of Grey novel with me

OR

Watch the movie with me?

WOULD YOU RATHER...

Have your butt squeezed

OR

Have it spanked?

Have sex with just one person watching

OR

50 people watching?

WOULD YOU RATHER...

Remain a virgin until marriage, and have the best sex life

OR

Stay unmarried and have unlimited number of sexual partners, with no commitment?

Grab boobs, if you were invincible

OR

Grab butts?